The Food Cycle

by David Smith, 1962-

Illustrations by John Yates

Thomson Learning • New York

Titles in the series

The Human Cycle
The Food Cycle
The Plant Cycle
The Water Cycle

Words printed in **bold** can be found in the glossary on page 30.

First published in the
United States in 1993 by
Thomson Learning
115 Fifth Avenue
New York, NY 10003

First published in 1993 by
Wayland (Publishers) Ltd.

Library of Congress Cataloging-in-Publication Data
Smith, David, 1962-
  The food cycle / by David Smith ; illustrations by John Yates.
    p.   cm. – (Natural cycles)
  Includes bibliographical references and index.
  Summary: Discusses the role food plays in our health, where
different foods come from, and how food is processed for sale
around the world. Includes scientific activities and projects.
   ISBN 1-56847-093-2 ; $12.95
   1. Food Juvenile literature. 2. Nutrition – Juvenile literature.
[1.Food. 2. Nutrition. 3 Food – Experiments. 4. Experiments.]
I. Yates, John, 1939-   ill. II. Title. III. Series.
TX355.S638   1993
641.3 – dc20   93-24391

Printed in Italy

Contents

Food for life

We all have favorite foods. Perhaps your favorite is chocolate, or ice cream. Maybe you prefer juicy fresh fruit. But food is more than something nice to eat. Our bodies need food. We cannot live without it.

Why do we need food?

Imagine your body is a factory. The **vital organs** inside you, such as your heart and lungs, are like the factory machines. The skin and bones of your body are like the bricks and cement of the factory walls, protecting the vital organs. The food you eat is the fuel that gives you the energy to keep the machines working. Food also supplies the building blocks needed to build a strong, healthy body.

We all need food to survive. Food gives us the energy to breathe and move – to live, in fact.

Have you ever thought how much fun it would be if you could eat just your favorite food . . . all day, every day? This might sound good, but nothing could be further from the truth. Your body must have a variety of different types of food, if you want to be healthy.

The food cycle

All living things need food: for growth, for damage repair, and for energy.

Plants make their own food by mixing different ingredients. They take in water and **mineral salts** from the soil and **carbon dioxide** from the air. The plants' green leaves trap light energy from the sun and use it to help turn the ingredients into sugars and **starches**, which are needed for energy and growth. This process of making food is called **photosynthesis**.

The food energy made by photosynthesis is passed on to animals when they eat plants. Some animals get their food by eating only plants. They are called herbivores.

ABOVE Most plants, like this beautiful sunflower, use energy from the rays of the sun to help make their own food. The plants' green leaves trap the energy from the Sun.

Sheep are herbivores. This means that they eat only plants.

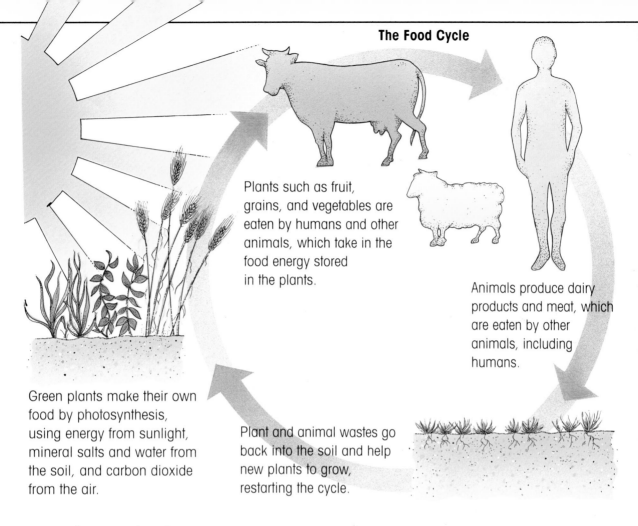

The Food Cycle

Plants such as fruit, grains, and vegetables are eaten by humans and other animals, which take in the food energy stored in the plants.

Animals produce dairy products and meat, which are eaten by other animals, including humans.

Green plants make their own food by photosynthesis, using energy from sunlight, mineral salts and water from the soil, and carbon dioxide from the air.

Plant and animal wastes go back into the soil and help new plants to grow, restarting the cycle.

Animals that feed on other animals are called carnivores. Humans can eat both plants and animals and are known as omnivores.

When plants and animals die, their remains are broken down and go back into the earth. The minerals and energy they were using when they were alive go back into the soil, too. These **nutrients** are taken up by plants and used to help them grow. In this way, the food cycle starts again.

BELOW Lions eat only other animals. They are known as carnivores.

7

What's in a meal?

The next time you eat a meal, take a look at the foods in front of you. Foods can be put into a few different groups. Every day we should try to eat foods from each group if we are to give our bodies everything they need to grow and stay healthy. Let's take a look at this packed lunch.

The whole-wheat bread of the sandwich contains carbohydrates and **fibe**r. The carbohydrates give us energy. Fiber helps to keep our digestive systems working well.

Bread, Cereals, Grain, and Pasta
Bread
Rice
Bran flakes
Spaghetti

Meat, Poultry, Fish, Beans, Eggs, Nuts
Lentils
Eggs
Tuna fish
Beef, lamb

Tuna fish

Orange Juice

The orange juice contains vitamin C, which helps to firm our skin and to keep our hair, eyes, and teeth healthy. It also helps to fight illness.

The tuna in the sandwich contains proteins. Proteins are used to build up our bodies. Meat, chicken, and beans contain protein, too.

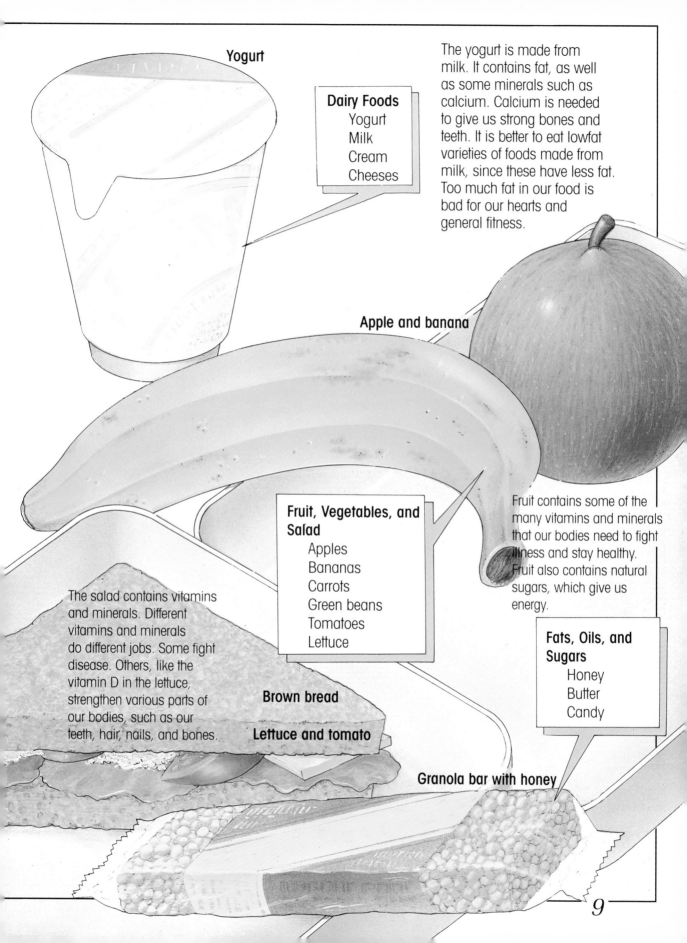

Yogurt

The yogurt is made from milk. It contains fat, as well as some minerals such as calcium. Calcium is needed to give us strong bones and teeth. It is better to eat lowfat varieties of foods made from milk, since these have less fat. Too much fat in our food is bad for our hearts and general fitness.

Dairy Foods
Yogurt
Milk
Cream
Cheeses

Apple and banana

Fruit contains some of the many vitamins and minerals that our bodies need to fight illness and stay healthy. Fruit also contains natural sugars, which give us energy.

Fruit, Vegetables, and Salad
Apples
Bananas
Carrots
Green beans
Tomatoes
Lettuce

The salad contains vitamins and minerals. Different vitamins and minerals do different jobs. Some fight disease. Others, like the vitamin D in the lettuce, strengthen various parts of our bodies, such as our teeth, hair, nails, and bones.

Brown bread

Lettuce and tomato

Fats, Oils, and Sugars
Honey
Butter
Candy

Granola bar with honey

9

Where in the world?

The food we eat comes from all over the world and is grown in many different **climates**. You can find out where different foods come from by reading food packaging labels and displays in supermarkets. This map shows the climates of different countries.

These sockeye salmon live in the cold waters off British Colombia.

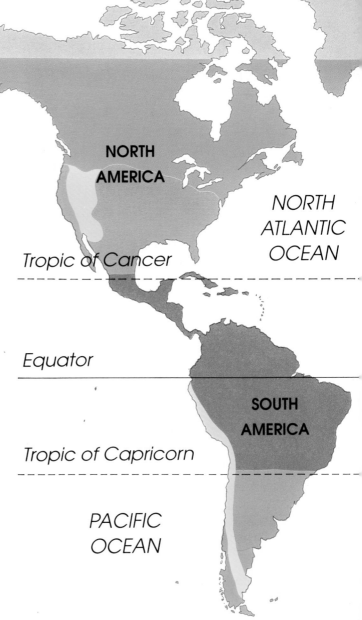

NORTH AMERICA

NORTH ATLANTIC OCEAN

Tropic of Cancer

Equator

SOUTH AMERICA

Tropic of Capricorn

PACIFIC OCEAN

KEY

Arctic lands

Cooler temperate lands

Warmer temperate lands

Deserts

Tropical lands

RIGHT These delicious red apples are grown in the cool temperate lands of northern Europe.

BELOW These dates are grown in the dry climate of Israel.

ARCTIC OCEAN

EUROPE

ASIA

AFRICA

PACIFIC OCEAN

INDIAN OCEAN

SOUTH ATLANTIC OCEAN

LEFT
The hot wet climate of Sri Lanka is ideal for growing tea.

11

Is it fresh?

These lemons are growing in Ojai, California. Usually lemons are picked when they are still slightly green and unripe. By the time they arrive in the stores they will be just ripe enough to use.

Most people in this country buy their food from grocery stores and supermarkets. There is an amazing selection to choose from. Before we buy food, a lot of effort is made to make sure it reaches us in the best possible condition.

Fresh foods are fruit and vegetables that have just been harvested, or meat from animals that have just been slaughtered (killed). It is healthy to eat fresh foods, when they are prepared

Garden peas, fresh from the pod! Freshly picked fruit and vegetables often have far more taste than those that have been frozen or canned. Food that has been canned also loses some of its nutrients.

Fungi in the air have caused the tangerine at the front of this picture to grow mold. Fruit and vegetables should be stored in a clean, dry place, in order to make them last.

properly, because they still contain all their natural food value and flavor.

However, as soon as plants have been harvested or animals have been slaughtered, they start to change. **Chemicals** inside them start to decay, and tiny living things called **bacteria** and **fungi** start to grow. These things can spoil the taste of the food. The bacteria and fungi also start to make toxins, or poisons, which could give us food poisoning if we ate them.

Using the cold

Food producers can do many things to make sure that fresh food is at its best when it reaches the stores. The truck in this picture is carrying meat. It is **refrigerated**, to keep the meat fresh until it reaches the store.

14

Bacteria and fungi spread quickly when food is kept in warm places. If the food is kept in colder conditions, the spread of decay and the growth of bacteria and fungi is slowed down. For this reason food is often transported, stored, and displayed in refrigerated containers.

Refrigeration does not keep food fresh for really long periods of time. Other methods are used to keep decay and bacteria from spoiling food. Freezing is an excellent way of keeping food unspoiled. It stops bacteria from growing and prevents decay by turning the water in food to solid ice. Food is frozen at **temperatures** between 20°F and −10°F. The lower the temperature, the longer the food will last. However, not all foods can be frozen. Some foods, such as tomatoes and lettuce, are damaged by the ice and are soft and shapeless when they thaw.

At home we can keep food fresh for longer by putting it in a refrigerator. Without refrigerators, we would have to shop for fresh food every day.

Using heat

The oldest way to preserve food uses heat from the sun. For thousands of years people have hung meat, fish, and sometimes fruit, to dry in the heat of the sun.

Canned foods are **preserved** using heat. Food is put in **sterile** cans, which are sealed and put under steam. The steam is very hot – about 250°F – and kills any bacteria. Sometimes the food is put into bottles or jars. The sealed containers protect the food from bacteria in the air. Food preserved in this way loses some of its food value. However, canned or bottled food can stay fit to eat for up to two years!

See for yourself

You will need some fruit, screw-top jars, sugar, salt, vinegar, water, teaspoons, and some plastic bags.

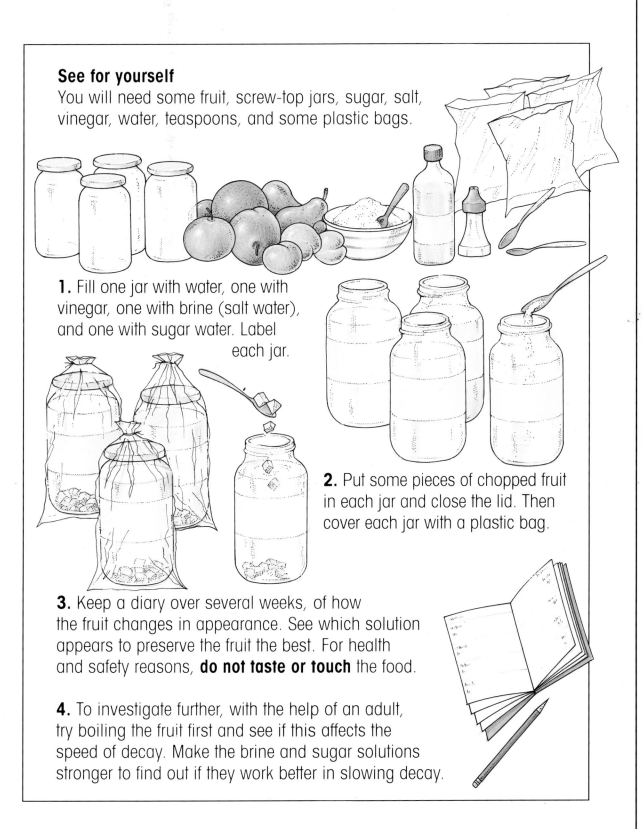

1. Fill one jar with water, one with vinegar, one with brine (salt water), and one with sugar water. Label each jar.

2. Put some pieces of chopped fruit in each jar and close the lid. Then cover each jar with a plastic bag.

3. Keep a diary over several weeks, of how the fruit changes in appearance. See which solution appears to preserve the fruit the best. For health and safety reasons, **do not taste or touch** the food.

4. To investigate further, with the help of an adult, try boiling the fruit first and see if this affects the speed of decay. Make the brine and sugar solutions stronger to find out if they work better in slowing decay.

Food additives

OPPOSITE These women are checking the quality of potato chips in the factory, before they are put into bags. Potato chips are a kind of processed food. You can find out which additives are added to them by checking the ingredients label on the bag.

BELOW All of this food has been processed in some way. This means that additives have been added to alter either the look, the taste, or the feel of the food.

Much of the food we eat is fresh and natural. This means that, when we buy it, the food has changed very little since it was harvested.

Other foods, like the ones in the picture below, are different. They have natural ingredients in them, but they are produced in factories by food companies. These foods have chemicals called additives in them.

All foods contain some natural chemicals. Additives, however, are chemicals that have been put into food by people.

Food additives do many jobs. Some are preservatives, which keep the food from spoiling. Others, such as sweeteners and flavorings, make the food taste different. Artificial colorings are used to make the food look brighter and more attractive.

Although additives often make food look and taste better, they often do not make the food more healthy. Some people prefer to eat natural food, since certain additives can be bad for us.

Preparing and cooking a meal

Preparing and cooking food is something only humans do. With imagination and a little effort we can come up with recipes that are both tempting and healthy. This delicious-looking milkshake has been made with fresh strawberries, lowfat milk and yogurt.

Cooking food to make a meal is something that only humans do. No other animal does this.

Cooking does several things to food. It makes some foods taste better and more pleasant to eat. Tough vegetables like potatoes and turnips are softened when they are cooked, and can be digested more easily.

Cooking food also helps to kill harmful bacteria. However, if food is cooked for too long, many of the nutrients it contains are also lost. It is a good idea to steam vegetables rather than boil them, since steaming destroys fewer nutrients. Some foods, such as fresh fruit or salads, are eaten raw, but they must be washed before they are eaten to remove dirt or chemicals.

LEFT Many vitamins and minerals are found just beneath the skin of fruit and vegetables. When we remove the skin by peeling, we also remove these precious nutrients.

BELOW Bacteria can breed very easily in a warm kitchen. It is very important to clean the kitchen regularly and to make sure that our knives, forks, spoons, and plates are clean too.

Keeping food clean is very important. Food should always be stored in a cool, clean, dry place before it is cooked. When we prepare food for cooking, we must make sure that the work surfaces and the knives we use are all clean, too.

Handling food this way is part of being **hygienic**. It is an important way to stop harmful bacteria from spreading disease, and it helps to keep us fit and healthy!

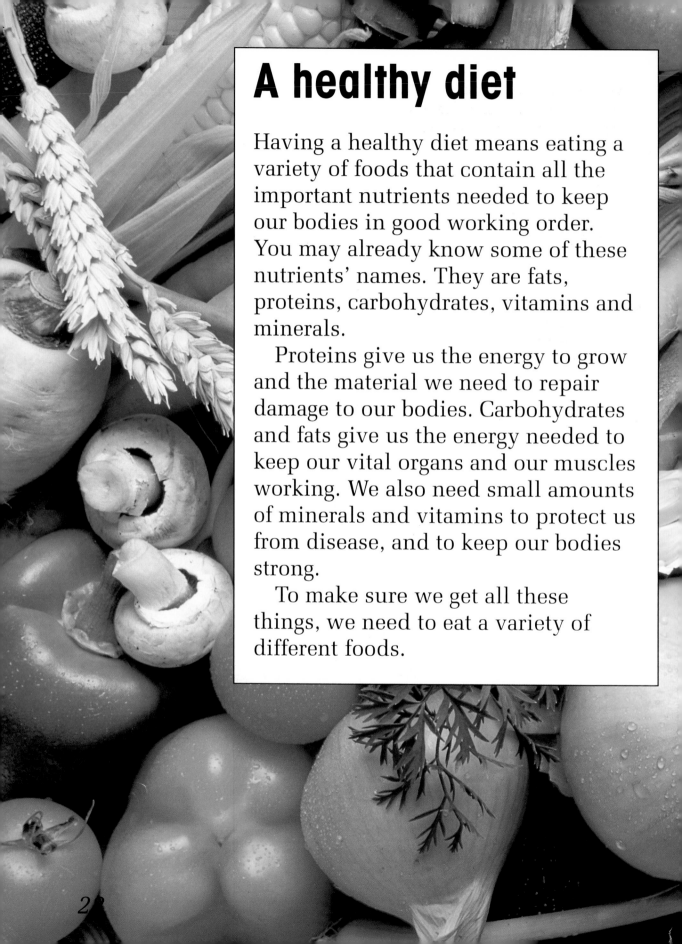

A healthy diet

Having a healthy diet means eating a variety of foods that contain all the important nutrients needed to keep our bodies in good working order. You may already know some of these nutrients' names. They are fats, proteins, carbohydrates, vitamins and minerals.

Proteins give us the energy to grow and the material we need to repair damage to our bodies. Carbohydrates and fats give us the energy needed to keep our vital organs and our muscles working. We also need small amounts of minerals and vitamins to protect us from disease, and to keep our bodies strong.

To make sure we get all these things, we need to eat a variety of different foods.

This picture shows how some of the most important nutrients in food are used and explains why our bodies need them.

Vitamin A is good for our eyes, bones, and teeth. The best foods for vitamin A are vegetables, particularly carrots.

Vitamin B helps to build a healthy blood supply. It is found in eggs, meat, and dairy produce.

Iron also helps our blood to stay healthy. Green vegetables such as cabbage and broccoli are excellent sources of iron.

Carbohydrates are dissolved by our bodies and can be turned into energy-giving glucose. Vegetables, pasta, and bread are good sources of carbohydrates.

Vitamin C is needed to keep our bones and skin healthy. It also helps us to fight illness. Citrus fruits such as lemons and oranges are a good source of vitamin C.

Calcium keeps our bones and teeth strong. Milk and green vegetables contain a lot of calcium.

Proteins build muscles and help our vital organs to stay in good repair. Fish, meat, beans, poultry, and dairy products are rich in protein.

Mouth watering!

OPPOSITE Look at this tasty burger! Think about biting into it. . . . Has your mouth started to water?

For most of us, sitting down to our favorite meal is something to look forward to, but what makes a meal our favorite?

Our senses play an important part in getting us ready to eat food. First of all, a meal has to look attractive and smell appetizing. The look and smell of food triggers off **glands**, which produce saliva in our mouths. When this happens we say that our mouths are watering. What is really happening is that our mouths are getting ready to receive food.

See for yourself
There are four groups of food tastes: bitter, sour, salty, and sweet. You can investigate how your sense of taste is linked to sight and smell.

You will need a selection of different foods (such as cheese, jam, apple, onion, yogurt, orange, tomato, chocolate, and lemon), some friends, and some plates and covers for the food.

1. Blindfold some friends and allow them to taste a small bite of each food, while holding their noses. See if they can name the foods and put them into taste groups.

2. Now try a second tasting using all the senses. See if they can put the foods into taste groups now.

25

Digestion

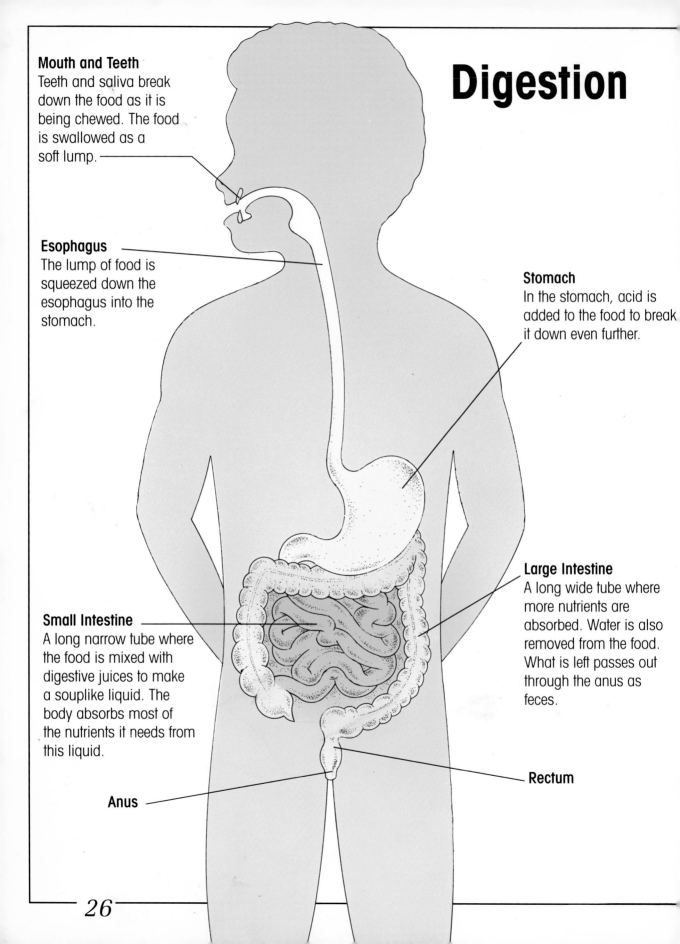

Mouth and Teeth
Teeth and saliva break down the food as it is being chewed. The food is swallowed as a soft lump.

Esophagus
The lump of food is squeezed down the esophagus into the stomach.

Stomach
In the stomach, acid is added to the food to break it down even further.

Small Intestine
A long narrow tube where the food is mixed with digestive juices to make a souplike liquid. The body absorbs most of the nutrients it needs from this liquid.

Large Intestine
A long wide tube where more nutrients are absorbed. Water is also removed from the food. What is left passes out through the anus as feces.

Anus

Rectum

Before your body can use the nutrients in your food to do important jobs, your meal must first be digested. This means that it is gradually broken down into tiny bits that your body can use. The parts of your body that do this job make up the digestive system. The breaking down of the food is called digestion.

Digestion starts as soon as food enters your mouth and you chew it. Digestion ends when the waste (the parts of the food your body cannot use) leaves your body through the **anus** when you go to the toilet. The passage from the mouth to the anus is called the digestive tract, or alimentary canal.

Food takes about twenty hours to travel all the way through the alimentary canal. As the food passes through, it is broken down into a soup-like liquid, and the important nutrients are **absorbed** into the body.

The digestive process starts as soon as food enters your mouth and you chew. Your teeth crush the food, while saliva starts to break it down even further.

The waste system

If you want to be fit and healthy it is essential that your digestive system work well. Eating plenty of fiber and exercising regularly will help to keep your digestive system in good working order.

Not all of the food we eat is used by our bodies. When digestion has finished, waste food passes along the large intestine and forms into **feces**. The feces collect in the **rectum**, before passing out of the body through the anus when we go to the toilet. The diagram of the digestive system on page 26 showed you where all these parts of the body are. The feces contain undigested food parts, food parts we do not need, and poisons, or toxins. It is important that your waste system work well, so that it there is regular removal of these wastes from your body.

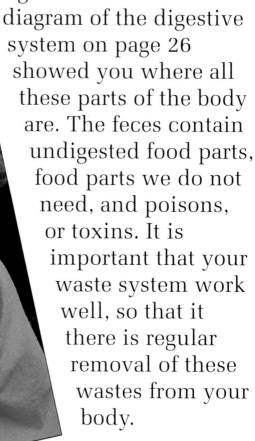

To help keep your waste system working properly, it is a good idea to eat plenty of foods that contain fiber. Fiber gives more bulk to the waste, helping it pass along the large intestine more easily.

Most liquid waste is passed through our **kidneys** and is stored in the **bladder**, until we need to go to the toilet. Our body gets rid of liquid waste as **urine**.

When fresh food is processed a lot of the fiber it contains is removed. Whole-wheat bread is made of flour that has not been processed. It still contains much of its fiber.

Glossary

Absorbed   Soaked up.

Anus   A small opening at the end of the large intestine, where solid waste leaves the body.

Bacteria   Very small organisms that are all around us. Some cause diseases.

Bladder   The part of your body that holds liquid waste (urine) until it is ready to leave your body when you go to the toilet.

Carbon dioxide   One of the many gases in the air. It is used by plants to make food.

Chemicals   The general scientific name for many of the different substances in the world around us.

Climate   The weather conditions in a place.

Feces   The solid waste that is produced when food is digested.

Fiber   Something found in food that our digestive system cannot break down. It passes right through the body and comes out in feces.

Food producers   All the people who are involved in making the food that you buy at the store.

Fungi   (singular, fungus) A group of living things similar to plants but that do not use sunlight to make their food.

Glands   Special parts of the body that produce important substances, such as saliva.

Hygienic   Clean.

Kidneys   A pair of vital organs in the body. Their job is to help get rid of urine that is made when your meal is digested.

Mineral salts   Substances that are needed to protect

our bodies and make them work well.

Nutrients Any of the things in food that are needed for health, such as minerals, proteins, and vitamins.

Photosynthesis The process by which green plants make food from light.

Preserved Kept from decaying.

Rectum The end of the alimentary canal.

Refrigerated Kept very cold. Refrigerated trucks and containers keep food cold, to keep it from decaying.

Starches Foods that plants make by photosynthesis.

Sterile Without germs.

Temperature The hotness or coldness of something.

Urine The liquid waste that is produced when food and drink are digested.

Vital organs All the important organs inside the body, such as the heart and lungs.

Further Reading

Burns, Marilyn *Good For Me! All About Food in 32 Bites.* New York: Little, Brown, 1978.

Davies, Kay and Oldfield, Wendy. *Food.* Starting Science. Austin: Raintree Steck-Vaughn, 1991.

Kerrod, Robin. *Food Resources.* The World's Resources. New York: Thomson Learning, 1993.

Patent, Dorothy H. *Where Food Comes From.* New York: Holiday House, 1991.

Reed-King, Susan. *Food and Farming.* Young Geographer. New York: Thomson Learning, 1993.

Swallow, Su. *Food for the World.* Facing the Future. Austin: Raintree Steck-Vaughn, 1991.

Picture acknowledgments
All Sport 23; Bruce Coleman 13, 16; Cephas 5, 6, 7; Eye Ubiquitous 16, 29; Images 28; Life File 25; Science Photo Library 4, 12, 23; Tony Stone 10, 11, 13, 19, 20; Swift 6; WPL 5, 21; Zefa 18; Zul Mukhida 15. The artwork on pages 10-11 is by Peter Bull.

Index